RELATIONSHIPS

Navigating the Left Bank

RELATIONSHIPS

TERRY CARROLL

OAKLAND HOUSE PRESS

OAKLAND, CALIFORNIA

"Plantzilla" (featured on page 102) is a tribute to
the most excellent children's book of that title,
written by Jerdine Nolen and illustrated by David Catrow,
published by Voyager Books (2002),
and imitated by only the most discerning young artists.

Design, layout, and pre-production
by Terry Carroll
using Adobe Photoshop and InDesign on a Dell desktop computer
Typeface: Adobe Garamond Professional

Printed in the U.S.A.
on 100-lb. Lustro Dull White Text
using a duotone separation with a 300-linescreen output
at The Stinehour Press
Lunenburg, Vermont
www.stinehourpress.com

Limited First Edition
(750 Copies)

396/750
Terry Carroll

Published and distributed by:
Oakland House Press
Ocean View Drive
Oakland, CA 94618-1535
Orders and inquiries:
510-287-6286
house@oaklandhousepress.com

Artist's Statement & Dedication

Relationships is a manifesto of innocence and understanding, love and friendship, romance and passion, curiosity and revelation.

I present this collection of photos for and because of Linda Dardarian. My first book, it goes to print on the twenty-fifth anniversary of that exuberant night we fell in love.

Terry Carroll
January 28, 2008
Oakland, California

Funeral at the Recoleta

Rick, Benched

Feeding Fowl

Taking in the Statehouse

View of Edinburgh

Rain Buckets at the Oakland Museum

Light and Mass

To the Top of the Lighthouse

Conner (Peek-a-Boo)

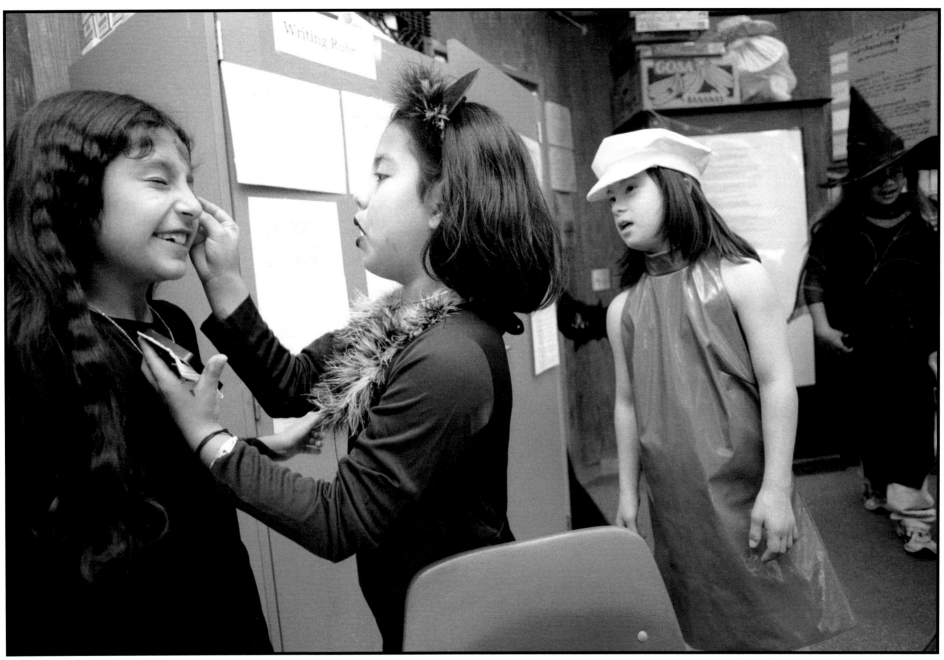

Preparing for the Halloween Parade

Miss Margaret Advises Rev. Dennis

The Skirt Fits Nicely

Flower Girl Tended To

The Return of Glamor

PRAGUE, 2000

Out, Holding Hands

Showing How It's Done

Diane Dancing

The Fan

Teen Mosh

Swingin'

Taking Flight in Maui

The Bride's Contingent

Running the Berm

A Bench for Each

Morning Roadside Washup

House Portrait

In Case of Emergency

Thanksgiving Day at the Stables

Brazilian Officers in Rome

Nine in a Line from Behind

Nine Hams Hanging

Lamb, Straight from the Lorry

Dog as Co-Pilot

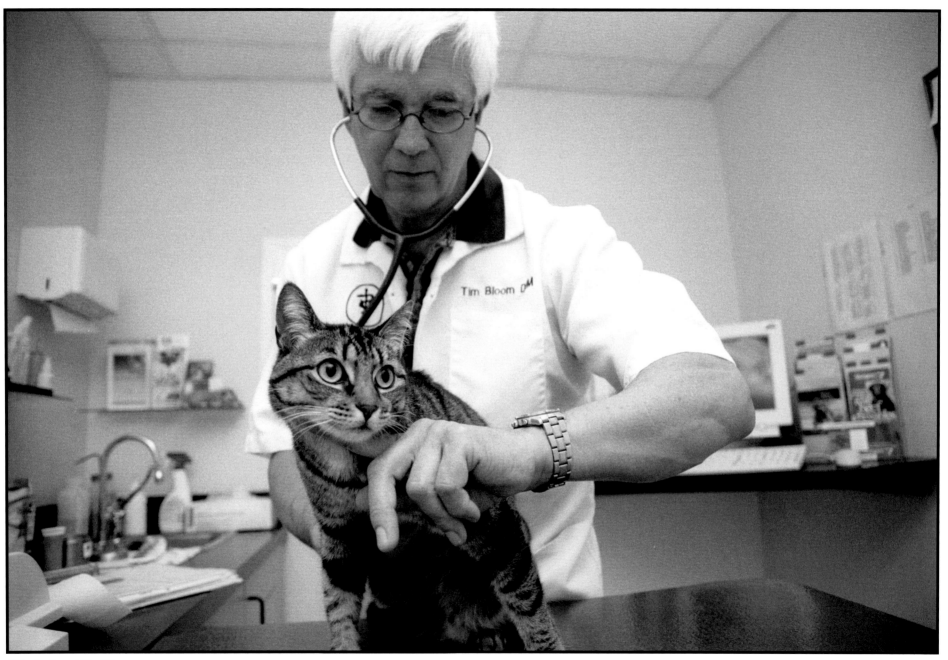

Elizabeth and Dr. Bloom

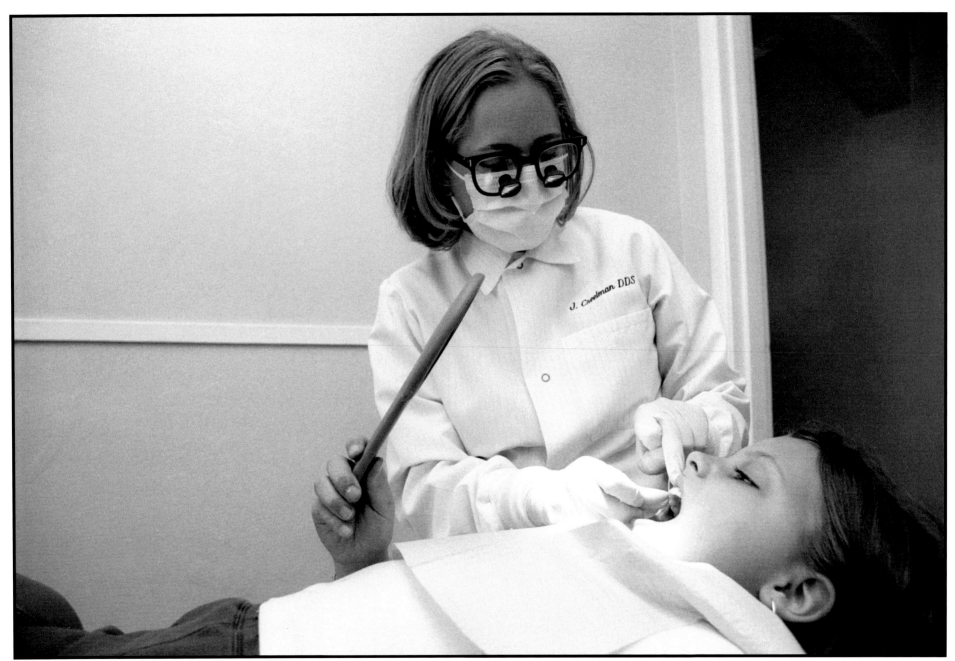

Dr. Creelman's Flossing Lesson

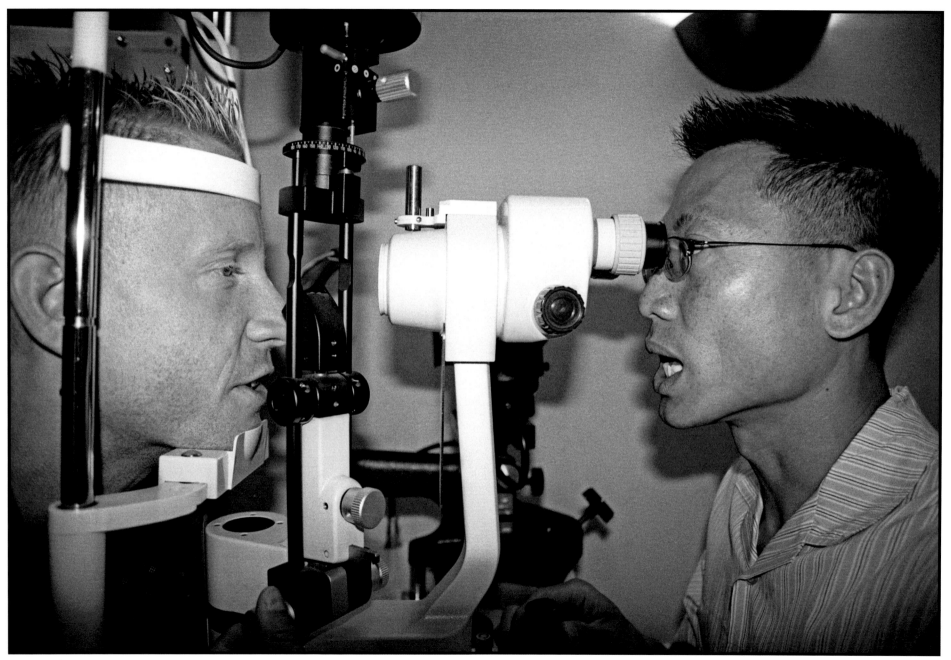

Eye Exam

Showing Grandson Around Manhattan

Fractions Made Whole

His First Boutonniere

After Posing with the Queen's Guard

Standoff

The Guitarist and the Clothier

Visiting Her Cat

Reviewing the Guard

Small Audience

Artistic License

Portraits of Shawnee

Goats Like Celery. Do They Like Little Girls?

BERKELEY, CALIFORNIA, 2007

Brought to His Attention

Fixing the Sidewalk, Cleaning the Window

New York City, 1987

Contending with Snow Monkeys

Non-Mutual Interest

Swordplay at La Defense

Framed

ROME, 2001

60

Access to the Polls

Daredevil

Scooters Are Number One

Spilled Pills

Impassioned Leader

Disorderly Procession

Managing the Crosswalk

The Liberty Belles Salute You

Girlfriends on Via Condotti

Pom-Pom Girls in the Rain

The Embrace

The Bride and the Photographer

We Were There

This Ring

Post-Parade Celebration

Majorettes for Peace

Brenda and Tom, Singing and Laughing

Sharon Needles and Robert T.

Face Paint Envy

Consuelo and Anna in the Park

Nan and Kitty Remember ...

FINTONA, NORTHERN IRELAND, 1995

81

On the Verge of Yes

Waiting for Something to Happen

Mark and Mrs. Pearl

In Love at Friends' Wedding

Berkeley, California, 1996

When Fifth Graders Visit Their Fourth-Grade Teacher

Friends at the Wedding

Cigarette and Swordfish

Two Poodles

The Farmer Comforts the Cowboy

Trigonometry

You're About to Be Photographed

Tied Tight at Opening

Gossip on Portobello Road

London, 2002

Purse Shop

Cup of Coffee and a Pair of Legs

Balloon Mime Gets No Break

Cab Driver Card Game

Mid-Performance Considerations

Jam Session at Peggy's

Clarinet Recital

Jonathan Poses with Robert (and Plantzilla)

Battery-Powered Lollies

Parliamentary Guards Crossing

Maybe a Swim

When the Castro Street Fair Was Young

Around the Fourth Wall

New Americans

Husbands and Sisters

All Quiet on Via del Orso

Just Married

Last-Minute Advice

Monique's Letter

The Groom and Sister June

Window Shopping by Bicycle

Paris, 2003

Education at the Orsay

A Lovely Day for Baby Ducks

Close Reading

Lena's Glow

Help Up the Stairs

Walkies After Work

Hitchhiking Highway 4

The Majorettes of Palombara Sabina

The Band Is Looking Up

Autograph Seekers

YANKEE STADIUM, 2002

125

Miles Explores Dynamic Earth

Startled Near Spitalfields

The Rant, Considered

We Are Not Criminals

The Bragging Trumpeter

Negotiated Protest

Dealer Called a Cheater

Cat Fight

Asleep in the Back Seat

Long Day for Young Gauchos

Shea's Awake

Sunday Inactivity

Paris Down There

Skateboarding at the Royal Exchange

Two Castles

Posing with the Temple

Friday Haircut

I was born in San Francisco in 1960, grew up in Martinez, California, and, except for a single year in Chico, California, I have lived my whole life in the Bay Area. I attended San Francisco State University, where I earned a bachelor's degree in creative writing in 1982 and a master's degree in American history in 1988. Then I taught for a while as an American history instructor at three different East Bay community colleges, before working in the legal field as a non-lawyer for a decade, followed by several years as an elementary school classroom volunteer. Employment-wise, I've done a lot of things, but I've never worked as a professional photographer.

And yet, despite far more education, training, and professional work with words, I've always been a much better photographer than writer. I learned pretty much everything I needed as a photographer at Alhambra High School in Martinez (Class of '78), and took it from there. For various reasons (which I still believe was for the best), I dropped my ambitions to be a professional photographer as soon as I hit college. I never took a college course in photography nor any kind of post-high-school photo workshop. Photography simply became my personal artistic outlet, and I didn't want any outside direction.

With photography, I've always emphasized two fundamentals: composition and timing. My sense of composition comes from the visual arts in general and landscape photographers in particular—most notably Ansel Adams and Edward Weston. Using their examples of how to place objects within a frame and what to do with light, I've tried to remain rigorous with my compositions. And yet, I compose almost unconsciously, finding vectors and patterns from the scene, grabbing horizontals and verticals, and lining them up in my viewfinder, quickly and efficiently.

That allows me to concentrate on timing, which I *also* don't concentrate on; I just let it happen—because timing is everything. Timing tells the story, specifically through the "telling moment," when relationships reveal themselves. To capture those telling moments, I've made use of my natural rhythm. I'm a drummer and a pretty good dancer. Situations have tempos, and I seem to have an autonomic ability to find the beats. I almost always hit on the upbeat, the "two" or the "four." That's when action is at its physical apex, which, emotionally, is the most *open* moment. So though my compositioning is influenced by photographers who use very, very, tedious, exacting methods, I'm a frame-a-scene, catch-the-moment kind of photographer.

Hubcap Wide-Angle

MARTINEZ, CALIFORNIA, 1975

Few moments caught in this book were preceded by me announcing that I was going to take a picture or by my asking permission to do so. (Want to *not* catch a telling moment? Make an announcement beforehand.) In turn, few of these images came from anything but my engagement with ordinary life. Everything outside of the Bay Area I took as a tourist; almost everything else I took as a guest, friend, audience, or participant—out and about, among and interacting with the people in the frame. I'm a huge fan of classic, mid-Century photojournalism. It was the monumental 1955 photo book, *The Family of Man*, which I first discovered as a seventh grader in 1972, that made me want to be a photographer. And the book's contributors—the great *Life* and Magnum photographers, et al.—permanently shaped my photo sensibilities, as well as my personal philosophy. Most of what I do with a camera is self-assigned pretend photojournalism.

I shoot black-and-white, hand-held, 35mm. I use a wide-angle lens almost exclusively, so I'm usually at an arm's length—or conversational distance—from my subject. The wide-angle perspective is both optical and emotional: providing an *expansive* and *intimate* view at the same time, which I love for the "you are there" sense it provides the viewer.

Having thus been engaging optically and emotionally with the world around me for more than thirty years, I needed to finally put my favorite, most representative, interim results between covers. Choosing a theme around which to select my images was easy: "relationships" is what I'm always observing (as I assume most people do)—following life's little narratives or occupying one's mind by making connections.

Speaking of connections, I need to thank many, many people. But choosing whom to thank is a lot harder than choosing images for a book. I've never had an actual personal mentor behind my photography; in fact, I can only count one full-time professional photographer among my friends. Since the early 1970s I've had countless people in my life who are interesting and creative, consumers and/or practitioners of the arts, from whom I've received inspiration, knowledge, and encouragement. So, rather than attempt to name them all, forgetting many (or filling many pages), or point out particular people for particular gratitude, and invariably skewing the list to recent years, I'm going to just say that I have a lot of deeply satisfying relationships in my life; it is in their honor that I present **Relationships**.